Photography for TEENS

Displaying the Shot

Photography   Volume   3

by Jason Skog

Content Consultant:
Kevin Jeffrey
Professional Photographer

COMPASS POINT BOOKS
a capstone imprint

Compass Point Books
1710 Roe Crest Drive
North Mankato, MN 56003

Editor: Jill Kalz
Designer: Ashlee Suker
Media Researcher: Svetlana Zhurkin
Production Specialist: Danielle Ceminsky

 This book was manufactured with paper containing
at least 10 percent post-consumer waste.

Library of Congress Cataloging-in-Publication Data
Cataloging-in-publication information is on file with the Library of Congress.
ISBN 978-0-7565-4491-1 (library binding)
ISBN 978-0-7565-4531-4 (paperback)

Image Credits:
Alamy: Jeff Greenberg, 42 (bottom); Ashlee Suker, 17 (bottom), 30 (insets); Capstone
Studio: Karon Dubke, 12, 13, 16, 20, 21, 23, 25, 27, 32, 33, 34, 35; Corbis: Kevin Dodge,
44; Dreamstime: Anna Khomulo, back cover (bottom), 10, Iodrakon, 36, Penywise, back
cover (top); iStockphoto: Joshua Hodge Photography, 43 (bottom right), Juanmonino,
28, 29, LdF, 43 (bottom left), narvikk, 37, quavondo, 42 (top), Sebastian Duda, back
cover (middle), 22, sturti, 43 (top), Tom Gufler, 8 (top); Jill Kalz, 18, 19, 26, 33–35
(photo of tulips); Picasa, 8 (bottom); Shutterstock: aggressor (pencil scribble),
throughout, corepics, 31, Elzbieta Sekowska, 41, Goodluz, 43 (middle right), Igor Sirbu
(frames), 30, Jason Cox, 7, Jason Stitt, 9, joyfull, 5, Kuzma, 4, Lusoimages, 15, Marco
Regalia, cover, Matthew Williams-Ellis, 43 (middle left), monalisha (dotted circle),
throughout, Monkey Business Images, 40, Natthawat Wongrat, 11, ntwowe, 1 (middle),
24, R. Gino Santa Maria, 6, Ryger (background texture), throughout; Svetlana Zhurkin,
cover (butterflies inset), 14, 17 (top), 38, 39

Printed in the United States of America in Stevens Point, Wisconsin.
102011   006404WZS12

Table of Contents

Introduction

You got the shot. In fact, you got a lot of shots. Now what?

Get them off your camera and play with them! Share them! Celebrate them!

Setting up your photographs takes thought, patience, and careful preparation. So does taking them. For this final stage of the process, don't slack off. Put just as much work into displaying your images as you did getting them, and you'll be amazed at the results. Digital is king for most hobbyists, so this book will focus on the tips, tricks, and tools you'll need if you're using a digital camera.

Take time to carefully decide how to best showcase your photos.

The large screens offered by desktop computers are usually best for photo-editing work.

The digital photography boom has spurred most amateur photographers to replace film labs and darkrooms with computers and printers. Not only does digital deliver faster results, you have more control over the end product than ever before. Simply upload your images to a computer. Then adjust them and print them out in a fraction of the time it would have taken you to go to the store to have your film developed and prints made.

The Computer

Whether it's a Mac or a PC, desktop or laptop, you'll need a computer to get started. One of the most important considerations when editing and printing photographs is screen size.

Desktop computers generally have larger screens than laptops. They give you a better view of your images and how they're affected by the changes you've made. But laptops can get the job done too. They now come in a variety of screen sizes, and most have enough storage and processing power to go toe-to-toe with the average desktop system.

Visit a computer store and see what screen size is most comfortable for you. Keep your budget in mind too.

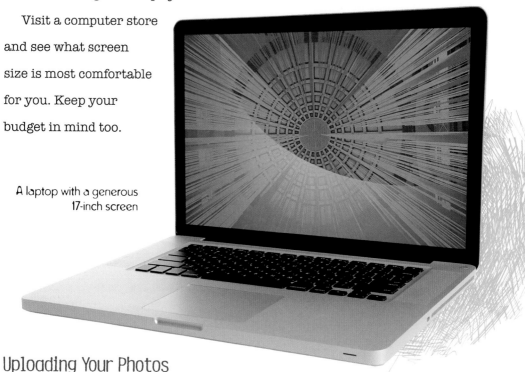

A laptop with a generous 17-inch screen

Uploading Your Photos

The first step in working with your photos is getting them off your camera and onto your computer. Most computers come with a basic photo-editing software program. Some digital cameras do too. There are also free photo-editing programs available on the Internet or through photo-sharing websites.

Check your computer for a slot that will accept your camera's memory card. If it has one, just remove the card from the

A SPACE OF YOUR OWN

Uploading, editing, and printing your photographs takes time and practice. Create a quiet, comfortable, and enjoyable work space for yourself—someplace permanent. That way you won't have to set up everything (and then put away everything) each time you want to work on your photos.

An ideal photo-editing and printing workstation should have space for your computer, keyboard, monitor, printer, and scanner (if you have one). It should also have a chair and shelves for reference books.

Some people prefer an L-shaped space. They place their chair on the short leg of the L and use the long leg as a large work space for framing or reviewing prints. A bright desk lamp and a natural light source from a window will also help you check your prints for proper color and cropping.

camera and place it in the slot. Uploading of your files should begin automatically. If your computer doesn't have one, see if your camera came with a cable. Use it to connect your camera to the computer's USB port. Uploading should start automatically, or the computer will ask whether you want to upload the images.

A cable enables you to upload photos directly from your camera to a computer.

Photo-Editing Software

Choosing photo-editing software can be overwhelming. Some photo software suites can be found online and downloaded for free. Others—such as the premium versions of Adobe Photoshop—can cost $1,000 or more. Programs such as Photoshop are loaded with advanced features designed to get the most out of every image and create professional-quality results.

If you're just starting out, save your money and get a taste for photo editing by downloading

Google offers a free photo-editing program called Picasa.

Picture this: You spent a whole weekend setting up your shots, taking them, and editing them until they're perfect. You think they're some of the best photos you've ever taken. You can't wait to share them. Then it happens. Your computer crashes. You lose everything. Game over. ACK!

Make a habit of saving your images to a back-up source—someplace off your computer. An external hard drive, a CD-R, or DVD disc are good choices. Even a high-capacity USB flash drive can hold a large number of photos.

Another option is to upload your images to a photo-sharing website. Just be sure you understand the terms of the site. Know whether the images will be saved forever or if they're at risk of being deleted after a certain amount of time.

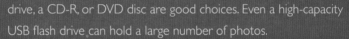

a free program first. Then if you find the program just won't let you accomplish what you want with your photos, you can always upgrade to a more expensive, professional version later. Some companies will let you download their software for free and use it for a limited time—a 30- or 60-day trial period, for example. If you like the program, pay for it, and it's yours to keep. If not, you can use it until the trial period expires.

PhotoScape is a free program you might try. It'll help you go from making basic prints to creating more advanced and detailed ones. Google's free Picasa photo-editing and sharing program is very easy to navigate. It includes most of the basic features amateur photographers would find useful.

The Printer

One area of technology that has advanced quickly—and affordably—is the inkjet printer. Less than 20 years ago, when inkjets were just hitting store shelves, they were relatively expensive. Their photo-printing quality was less than spectacular. Images looked fuzzy and smudgy, and colors were usually inaccurate.

Today's home-printed photos often match the quality of those printed in a store.

Today, however, many inkjet printers cost less than $100 and can produce images that are as good as most anything from a store photo lab. Paired with the right photo paper, inkjet printers can yield awesome images—ones you'd be proud to hang on your wall.

Still, printer quality can vary. A printer's resolution is measured in dots per inch. Inkjet printers spray almost microscopically small dots of ink on paper to create an image. Printers with a higher dpi number have a more dense ink pattern that will create prints with more detail and clarity. And printers with six colors, rather than four, generally produce more pleasing, lifelike prints.

Four-color inkjet printers mix black, cyan, magenta, and yellow to create all the colors in a photo.

But don't get too caught up in the numbers game. Some manufacturers' claims about dpi figures can be misleading. The best thing is to go to your local computer or office supply store and have a salesperson print some test photos for you. Then compare the results yourself. Be sure the tests are run on inkjet photo paper, not regular office paper. It will make a difference.

STEP 1

Start with a low-end, four-color inkjet printer. Note the dpi, and print a test photo on photo paper. How sharp or crisp does the image look?.

STEP 2

Next print a test photo from another four-color printer, one with a higher dpi. How does it compare to the first test photo? Any change in sharpness or color?

STEP 3

Now try printing from a six-color printer with about the same dpi. Does the quality of the image change? If so, how?

Paper and Ink

A good inkjet printer will help you create beautiful photos, but only if you invest in special inkjet photo paper. That's key. Regular office paper is fine for printing letters and homework. But using plain office paper for pictures leads to flat, lifeless photos with blurred, blended, or inaccurate colors.

Special photo paper is available in any office supply store, camera store, or "big box" store such as Walmart or Target. Paper comes in various sizes and finishes. Depending on your printer size and feeder tray, choose 4-by-6-inch, 5-by-7-inch, or 8-by-10-inch paper. You can opt for borderless paper or paper that includes a thin, white border around the edges.

Quality paper is key to getting the sharpest, richest photos from your printer.

From flat to matte to semigloss and glossy, photo paper finishes will also affect the final image. None are necessarily right or wrong, though some photos may look better with one finish versus another, depending on the image. In the end, it's like ice cream. Some people prefer chocolate. Others like vanilla. You decide which paper is right for you.

Some inks require a certain type of photo paper, and some photo papers respond only to certain inks. The two main types of inks are dye-based and pigment-based. Dye-based inks generally produce brighter, more vivid images that will last longer and aren't prone to fading. However, dye-based inks require longer drying times, making them prone to smudging. They require careful handling. Pigment-based inks are far more common because of their rapid, almost instant drying times. Be sure you know what kind of ink your printer uses before purchasing paper.

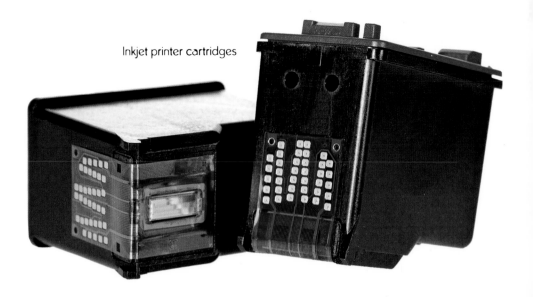

Inkjet printer cartridges

Chapter 2

Editing and Tweaking

Easily weed through your photos by viewing them in thumbnail or icon mode.

Once you've uploaded your images to your computer, it's time to take a spin through them to sort the "good" from the "bad and ugly." And don't worry if your bad and ugly shots outnumber your good ones, especially when you're just starting out. Rarely will all the photos you've taken be worthy of printing and preserving. Automatically delete images that are blurry, poorly lit, badly composed, or simply weren't what you were going for. Keep only the real gems—or at least the diamonds in the rough.

The great thing about digital photography is that you get to select and improve your favorites and print only those you want to keep. With film photography, you often would develop the film and have all of them printed, only to be stuck with those that didn't turn out—whether they were blurry, or your brother's eyes were closed, or your cat suddenly turned its head the other way.

With digital photography, blurry or too-dark shots can be deleted immediately.

No matter how hard you work to get a photograph right when you're taking it, sometimes when you get it up on your computer, something looks wrong. Maybe there's an element that's distracting from your subject. Maybe the color of the sky is off, or a face has an odd shadow falling across it. Think back to how you remember the scene in real life. What made you want to take the picture in the first place? What were you trying to accomplish? If something feels wrong in the image on your computer, rest assured. You can often fix it with a photo-editing program.

Although photo-editing tools can work a lot of magic, they can't save badly blurred photos.

Cropping and Resizing

What you capture in the camera frame isn't what you have to live with. Cropping a photo involves choosing the portion of the photo that you like most and eliminating the portion you like least. In some cases you can crop out distracting elements in the background or sides of your subject. You can even crop out unwanted people or objects. You can take a horizontal photograph and crop it so that it becomes vertical, and vice versa.

Cropping an image also means resizing it from the original file. Depending on your original file size, resizing can lead to some unwanted fuzziness in the final image. In that case use the sharpening tool in your photo-editing program to restore some clarity to the image.

Cropping allows you to focus on the important part of an image.

STEP 1

Pull up the image you want to crop onscreen.

STEP 2

Click on the cropping tool. Some programs allow you to trace, free-style, around the part of the photo you want to keep. Others have more rigid, rectangular crops.

STEP 3

After cropping, check the image for clarity. Does it look fuzzy? If so, use the sharpening tool included in most photo-editing programs.

THE DREADED RED EYE

Many digital cameras have a red-eye reduction feature. Before taking the picture, the camera shines a bright light on the subject. This burst of light shrinks the size of the person's pupils and reduces the likelihood of a red circle reflecting from the center of his or her eyes. But sometimes the feature is accidentally turned off or doesn't work quite the way it's supposed to. Most photo-editing programs have a red-eye correction feature to handle those cases. Clicking on the feature will do one of two things: It will detect the red spots automatically or bring up a small circle on your mouse arrow that you place over the spots yourself. Click. Fixed. Done.

Adjusting the Contrast

If your image appears too dark, try increasing the fill light or adjusting the contrast with your photo-editing software. Increasing the fill light will boost the light in darker portions of the photograph, bringing a subject's shadowy face into view. But it also increases the brightness throughout the photo, which can wash out details in brighter areas. Adjusting the contrast can help balance the light and dark areas of a photograph. Don't be afraid to play with these features until you get the effect you're looking for.

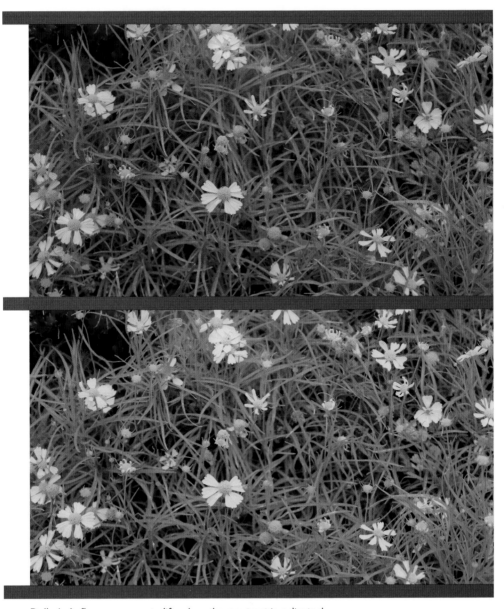

Dull, drab flowers come to life when the contrast is adjusted.

Color and Tint

It's a pretty basic thing, but in your image, greens should look green, reds should look red, and blues should look blue. So why does your dad's red shirt look pink? And your white dog blue? If you aren't happy with the colors you see onscreen, use the color adjusting tool, sometimes called auto color. It selects a neutral gray or white portion of the photograph and adjusts the red, blue, and green levels—the primary colors—to more natural levels. You may even consider tweaking the colors onscreen again once you print the photo on paper.

Straighten Up

There are times when a tilted image can look cool. An extreme tilt portrait, for example, can seem edgy and more spontaneous than a standard horizontal or vertical shot. But for tilts that aren't intentional, the resulting photos can feel off-balance. Correct this by using the "straighten" feature or tilt option included in most photo-editing programs. Simply rotate your image to correct any angle or imbalance.

Adjusting a tilted photo is easy with the straighten feature included in most photo-editing programs.

FUN WITH SPECIAL EFFECTS

Most photo-editing programs include a number of extra features that let you create fun and interesting effects with your photos. You can make pictures appear as though they are paintings. Add a soft focus and create a more soothing effect. Change them to a sepia tone for an old-fashioned feel. Add speech balloons. You can even pull, stretch, or squish your images into funny and scary shapes. Make a copy of your original file so you can preserve it if you don't like how your changes turn out.

IF YOU'RE GOING TO CONTINUE THIS ...

... WE'RE GOING TO HAVE PROBLEMS!

Retouching

You took the most amazing picture of your cousin, but you found
a small pimple on her chin when you uploaded the picture to
your computer. Bummer. Think the shot is ruined? Don't worry.
You can fix it.

The retouch feature is standard on most photo-editing suites.
It's almost like waving a magic wand.

BASIC BLACK AND WHITE

Just because you shot something in color doesn't mean you have to
keep it that way. In some cases the photo might be more dramatic
as a black-and-white image. Your photo-editing program provides a
feature that can swap color for black and white. Black-and-white photos
look best where there are striking dark and light areas. You may have
to adjust the contrast or white levels. But
changing to black and white can result
in a more pleasing, less distracting
image that lets the viewer
focus on the subject rather
than the colors.

STEP 1

Pull up the image you want to retouch onscreen. Here we want to remove the smudge on our subject's shirt.

	Spot Healing Brush Tool	J
	Healing Brush Tool	J
	Patch Tool	J
	Red Eye Tool	J

STEP 2

Click on the retouching tool and select a size, if applicable. The tool will usually appear as a circle. Select an unblemished area near the portion you wish to retouch and click on it. Doing so will "collect" material with which to cover the spot or smudge.

STEP 3

Now move the tool over the spot you want to erase, and watch it disappear! Ta daa! Clean shirt!

Framing, Sharing, and Storing

The same subject takes on a different mood, depending on its frame.

If you've gone to the trouble of taking a great photograph, carefully uploading and editing it on your computer, and then printing it, it's probably worth displaying. And not just on the refrigerator!

Mounting, Matting, and Framing

Your best work deserves the full treatment—mounting, matting, and framing. Most hobby stores carry everything you'll need to get the job done. Try doing it yourself, or take your photos to a professional frame shop and have them do it for you. It depends how hands-on you want to be and what sort of budget you have.

WORKING IN THE DARK

Before inkjet printers started popping up in people's homes, photographers had a choice: They could take their film to a processor to have the film developed and prints made; or they could build their own darkroom at home and do it themselves.

Home darkrooms grew in popularity among amateur photographers from the 1950s through the 1990s. Equipment and chemicals became increasingly easy to find, and the once-high prices dropped. However, the process remained delicate and tedious. Temperatures of the chemicals for developing film had to be precise and the timing just so. The same precision had to be applied for making prints. And if somebody accidentally opened a door or turned on a light, an afternoon's worth of work could be ruined in a blink. Darkroom processing took patience and care.

Because of the digital and inkjet revolution, most amateur photographers today have abandoned their darkrooms. Still, some remain, and a few diehards who have perfected their craft and art wouldn't have it any other way.

STEP 1

To mount your photo, start with a piece of mount board or foam-core display board.

STEP 2

Affix the photo to the board with a spray adhesive specially designed for photos. Spray the back of the photo in a sweeping motion, according to the directions.

You can also attach your photos with special two-sided tape or a dry adhesive paper that goes between the photo and the mounting board. Use whatever you're most comfortable with.

STEP 3

Carefully lay the photo on the board by putting down one edge and slowly rolling down the rest.

STEP 4

Use a rubber print roller to smooth evenly from the center of the photo to the edges. If you don't have a roller, simply cover the photo with waxed paper and drag a credit card across it, from the center to the edges.

continued on next page

STEP 5

Using a metal straight edge and a sharp utility knife, very carefully cut away the excess board.

STEP 6

Once the photo is properly mounted, add a mat. A mat is a border of thick cardboard that provides an additional framing element and a little visual distance between the photo and the frame itself. Available in every color imaginable, mats can provide a striking complement to your picture. Choose classic white or pull out a color from the photo.

STEP 7

Finally, frame your photo. The frame will depend on the size, shape, and kind of photo you have. Frame to the photo, not to the room you're going to put it in. Consider whether the frame will add to the image or distract. Is it the right color and style given the image you have and the tone you're trying to convey?

Cool, Dark, and Dry

If you're not going to put your finished photos on a wall, but you want them to last as long as possible, there are some tips. Extreme temperatures and changes in temperatures can damage photo paper and the ink that's printed on them. Pick a place that has a fairly stable temperature. Between 50 and 70 degrees Fahrenheit (10 and 21 degrees Celsius) is good, but the cooler side of that is even better.

A programmable thermostat ensures a safe temperature for your photos.

Humidity—the level of moisture in the air—is another concern. Too much humidity can cause photos to gather moisture and mold. Too little can cause them to become dry and brittle. A relative humidity of 35 to 45 percent is best.

Perhaps a photograph's biggest enemy? Sunlight. Take care to store your pictures in an area where they won't be exposed to the sun's harsh rays.

NOTHING LASTS FOREVER

As fun and convenient as printing your photos from home can be, there are some limitations to consider. Unlike conventional photo paper and processing, the ink used in inkjet printing is prone to fading—or disappearing altogether—over time. Images can fade and wash out in as little as five years, even under ideal conditions. While printer companies are working to improve the longevity of their inks, nothing compares to regular photo processing over the long haul. Have your most prized shots professionally processed if you want to help ensure a longer life for them.

Scrapbooks and Photo Albums

Photo albums and scrapbooks are an excellent way to preserve and later revisit some of your favorite shots.

Albums have clear plastic pages with sleeves for each photo, allowing you to flip through them like a book. Photo albums are a simple way to store hundreds of photographs while still providing easy access.

The variety of scrapbooking papers, decorations, and tools is endless.

Scrapbooks allow for more variety and creativity. Scrapbooks are bound pages of paper on which you can mount photographs individually and then add your own descriptions, mementos, stamps, stickers, and other decorations. Many hobby stores provide scrapbook supplies that can help you add another layer of interest to your favorite photos.

OFF THE WALL!

Photos displayed in a frame on the wall or on your computer screen are great, but what if you want them to be a bit more functional? Take that photo of your dog or you and your best friend and put it on a mug. Or a T-shirt. Or a mouse pad. Turn the photo you took of the Grand Canyon into a puzzle for your grandma's birthday. Blankets, key chains, jewelry, ornaments, tote bags, calendars, playing cards ... all of these items can be customized with photos you shot.

One way to get started is to visit an online photo service site such as Snapfish, Shutterfly, or Vistaprint. Upload your photo, and play with the site's easy-to-use tools to create any number of awesome products. If you'd feel more comfortable having someone walk you through the process, ask a salesperson at the photo-developing department of a "big box" store such as Walmart or Target for help. Those stores usually offer the same types of customizable photo items as online sites do. So do many supermarkets and drugstores with photo departments.

Want to be a little more hands-on? Office supply stores carry printable fabric transfers that are compatible with most home printers. Instructions usually refer you to a website where you can download special templates. Drop your image into the template, make any necessary printer adjustments, and you're set!

September

Elephant Adventure

But what if you're not super-crafty? In that case, upload your images to an online scrapbooking site! Choose from themed templates, or design your own. Customize your pages with digital stickers and other embellishments, add text, change background colors and textures. Most sites allow you to upload your photos, create an online scrapbook, and share it with friends for free. However, if you want to print out your finished pages, there's usually a fee. Be sure to read all site agreements thoroughly before starting any online project.

Unlike traditional scrapbooking, online scrapbooking doesn't require a large work space.

MAKING OLD PHOTOS NEW AGAIN

Got old family photographs that are torn, creased, or faded? With a scanner and some basic photo-editing tools, you can breathe new life into them. Just. Like. That.

Simply scan the old picture into your computer. Then remove creases, tears, or stains with the retouching tool, taking samples from the area around the damaged portion and replacing them with parts that are intact. For faded photos, adjust the contrast or alter the brightness.

When you're satisfied with the results, save the image to your computer and print a copy. With a little practice, you can restore old photos so they look like they were taken just yesterday.

MILK, BREAD, AND PHOTOS

If you don't have access to a computer or printer at home, many grocery stores and drugstores have self-serve photo kiosks. These booths accept your camera's memory card or a photo CD. You can adjust your photos and print them out right on the spot, usually for less than a dollar each.

Photo-Sharing Websites

The combination of digital photography and the Internet means that never before have so many photos been available for so many people to see from so many different locations. Today you can share photos on Flickr, Photobucket, or Snapfish. Upload to Picasa web albums, Tumblr, or your own personal website.

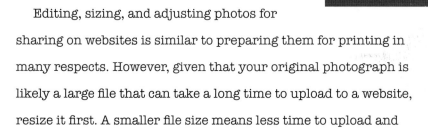

Editing, sizing, and adjusting photos for sharing on websites is similar to preparing them for printing in many respects. However, given that your original photograph is likely a large file that can take a long time to upload to a website, resize it first. A smaller file size means less time to upload and less time for it to load onscreen for viewers.

A big note of caution: Do not upload anything to a photo-sharing website that is potentially embarrassing, damaging, dangerous to yourself or others, or something you might regret later. In fact,

it's usually a good idea to wait a day before posting an image, just to give yourself a little time to think. Even if you decide to remove it later, somebody else can copy it in the meantime and re-post it, keeping it circulating forever.

SHOW THEM OFF

Congrats. You did it. You saw something funny, sweet, powerful, or magical. You thoughtfully set it up in your camera frame and shot it, tweaked it to perfection, and turned it out into the world. Other people liked it, but the best part is that you liked it too.

No two people see life exactly the same way. Share your vision. Connect. That's what photography is all about.

GLOSSARY

contrast—the difference between the lightest and darkest parts of an image

crop—to trim

darkroom—a room with no light, for developing film

flash drive—a small memory stick used to store or transfer data; also called a jump drive or thumb drive

matte—without shine or gloss

mount—to attach for display

port—an opening by which a computer is connected to another device, such as a printer

resolution—a measure of sharpness or clarity

FURTHER READING

Darlow, Andrew. *301 Inkjet Tips and Techniques: An Essential Printing Resource for Photographers.* Boston: Thomson Course Technology PTR, 2008.

Fitzgerald, Mark. *Photoshop CS4 After the Shoot.* Indianapolis: Wiley Pub., 2009.

Sholin, Marilyn. *The Art of Digital Photo Painting: Using Popular Software to Create Masterpieces.* New York: Lark Books, 2009.

Steinmueller, Uwe, and Juergen Gulbins. *Fine Art Printing for Photographers: Exhibition Quality Prints with Inkjet Printers.* Santa Barbara, Calif.: Rocky Nook, 2008.

ON THE WEB

Use FactHound to find Internet sites related to this book. All of the sites on FactHound have been researched by our staff.

Here's all you do:

Visit *www.facthound.com*

Type in this code: 9780756544911

ABOUT THE AUTHOR

Jason Skog has written several books for young readers. He is a freelance writer and former newspaper reporter living in Brooklyn, New York, with his wife and two young sons.

SELECT BIBLIOGRAPHY

Canfield, Jon. *Print Like a Pro: A Digital Photographer's Guide.* Berkeley, Calif.: Peachpit Press, 2006.

Daly, Tim. *Digital Print Styles Recipe Book: Getting Professional Results with Photoshop Elements and Your Inkjet Printer.* Berkeley, Calif.: Peachpit Press, 2009.

Doeffinger, Derek. *The Magic of Digital Printing.* New York: Lark Books, 2006.

Farrell, Ian. *Digital Photography Beyond the Camera.* Cincinnati, Ohio: David & Charles Ltd., 2007.

Look for all the books in the Photography for TEENS series:

INDEX